Everything Jacob Zuma Knows About HIV/Aids Prevention

Knowl Itall

Everything Jacob Zuma Knows About HIV/Aids Prevention

Everything Jacob Zuma Knows About HIV/Aids Prevention

Everything Jacob Zuma Knows About HIV/Aids Prevention

Knowl Itall

Knowl Itall

Knowl Itall

Knowl Itall

·